United States
Department of
Agriculture

Forest
Service

Northern
Research Station

General Technical
Report NRS-43

SOLVE
The Performance Analyst
for Hardwood Sawmills

Microsoft Windows® Edition

Jeff Palmer, Jan Wiedenbeck,
and Elizabeth Porterfield

Abstract

SOLVE is a computer program that assists sawmill managers in improving efficiency and solving problems commonly found in hardwood sawmills. SOLVE provides information on key operational factors including log size distribution, lumber grade yields, lumber recovery factor and overrun, and break-even log costs. With this information, sawmill managers can determine what types of logs (species, grades, and sizes) are affordable and predict the product yield from those logs.

The Authors

JEFF PALMER is an information technology specialist with the U.S. Forest Service, Northern Research Station, in Princeton, WV. He received a B.S. in business management and computer science from Bluefield State College in Bluefield, WV. He joined the Princeton, WV, research team in 1991.

JAN WIEDENBECK is a research forest products technologist with the U.S. Forest Service, Northern Research Station, in Princeton, WV. She received a B.S. in forestry from the University of Michigan in 1980, an M.S. in forest products from Virginia Polytechnic Institute and State University in 1988, and a Ph.D. in forest products from VPI in 1992. From 1981 to 1986 she was employed by Crown Zellerbach, Inc., as a forester and supervisor of sawmill quality control and production. She joined the U.S. Forest Service's Princeton, WV, research team in 1994.

ELIZABETH PORTERFIELD is an information technology specialist with the U.S. Forest Service, Northern Research Station, in Princeton, WV. She received a B.S. in computer science and mathematics from Concord University in Athens, WV. She joined the Princeton, WV, research team in 1988.

Acknowledgments

We would like to thank the following people who contributed to the improvement of the SOLVE program and this publication: Melody Cochran, Nicole Engeman, Katie King, Jessica McClung, Edward Thomas, and Frederica Wood.

We also wish to thank Paul Frederick (Wood Utilization Forester, Vermont Department of Forests, Parks and Recreation) for facilitating and organizing SOLVE workshops and for providing valuable feedback and support for the SOLVE project.

We further wish to extend special recognition and gratitude to Edward Adams (U.S. Forest Service, retired), who initially developed the SOLVE application.

Cover photo: Courtesy of Allegheny Wood Products. Log deck located at the Allegheny Wood Products facility in Princeton, WV.

CONTENTS

INTRODUCING SOLVE:
THE MICROSOFT WINDOWS® EDITION

The Microsoft Windows® edition of SOLVE is a substantial update of the previous Microsoft Access version of SOLVE-2003 and PC-SOLVE III. The earlier SOLVE programs were written between 1970 and 1995 by Ed Adams, who retired from the U.S. Forest Service in 1995. The SOLVE-2003 program was initially developed under a grant from the Forest Service's Economic Action Program of the Northeastern Area, which was awarded by the Vermont Division of Forestry. An earlier version of Vermont's SOLVE program, Micro-SOLVE, was released in 1986. The current version of SOLVE still uses Microsoft Access as its underlying database. If users do not have Microsoft Access 2000 installed on their systems, they can install the royalty-free copy of Microsoft Access 2000 Runtime, which is included on the SOLVE setup disk. When installed, Microsoft Access 2000 Runtime will function as the underlying database for SOLVE.

SYSTEM REQUIREMENTS

To use SOLVE, you will need the following:

- IBM compatible PC with the Microsoft Windows 2000 Professional or XP Professional operating system installed

- Microsoft Access 2000 (if you do not have MS Access 2000, you can use the free copy of MS Access 2000 Runtime included on the installation CD)

- Microsoft Snapshot Viewer Version 10 or above (included on the installation CD)

- 342 megabytes of available hard disk space for program installation

- Color VGA (or super VGA) monitor with a resolution of at least 1024 x 768 pixels

- CD-ROM drive

- Mouse or compatible pointing device

- Internet connection (for viewing the help files)

You will also need the following software for viewing online documents:

- Microsoft Internet Explorer (version 6 or better)

- Adobe Reader (you can download a free copy from the Adobe Web site: www.adobe.com/products/acrobat/readstep2.html)

INSTALLING SOLVE TO YOUR COMPUTER

If your computer does not allow you to install programs, then the SOLVE installation should be performed by a user or administrator who has administrative rights and privileges to your computer. The lack or absence of administrative rights may cause installation errors. Before running the setup program, make sure that your system's default font size is set to "Small fonts" for Windows 2000 systems or to "Normal" for Windows XP systems (Fig. 1). In Windows 2000 use the following steps to adjust your system's default font size:

- Open the *Control Panel* and select the *Display* icon.
- Select the *Settings* tab and click the *Advanced* button near the bottom of the dialog box.
- Select the *General* tab and set the *Font Size* to "Small Fonts."
- Click the *Apply* button to accept the changes.

To change the system font size for Windows XP, use the following steps:

- Open the *Control Panel* and select the *Display* icon.
- Select the *Appearance* tab and set the *Font size* to "Normal."
- Click the *Apply* button to accept the changes.

For more information on changing your computer's system settings, refer to your users guide or Microsoft Windows operating system manual.

To install SOLVE onto your computer, place the setup CD into your computer's CD-ROM drive. If the setup program does not start automatically, click on *Start* from the task bar and select *Run*. Enter "D:\SETUP.EXE" (or your CD-ROM's drive letter, if different from "D"). As you navigate through SOLVE's setup utility, you will be asked to specify a directory to install the application in (Fig. 2). You may use the default location given by the setup utility or specify a different location. After you have completed the installation procedure, be sure to shut down and restart your computer.

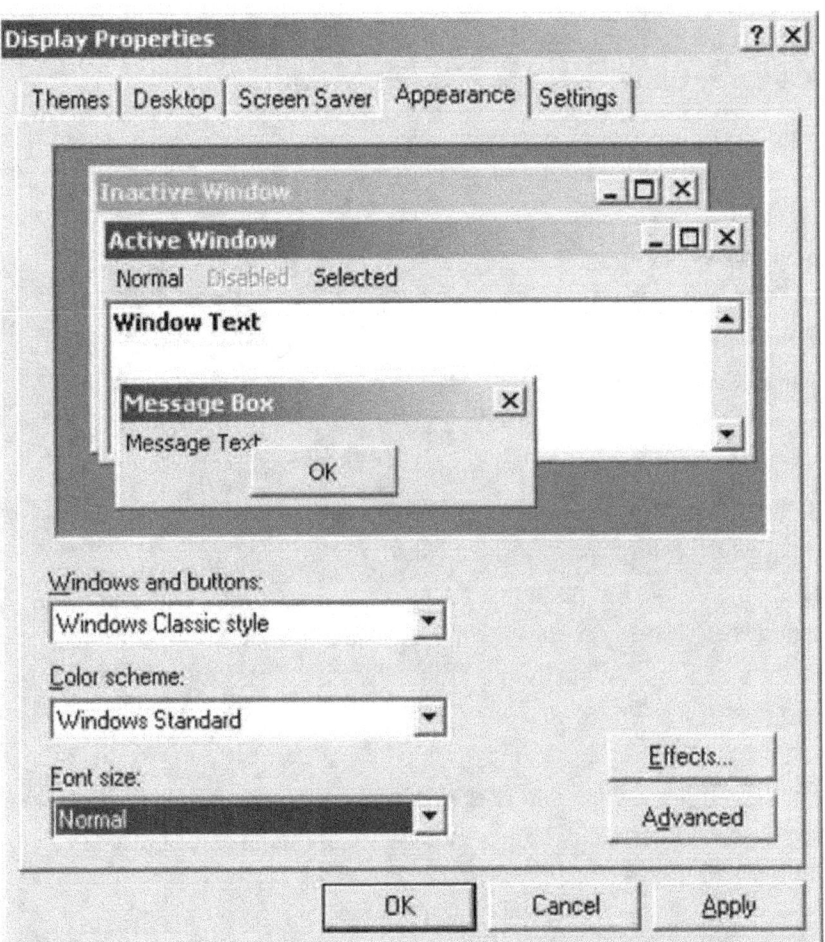

Figure 1.—The *Display Properties* dialog box for Microsoft Windows XP systems.

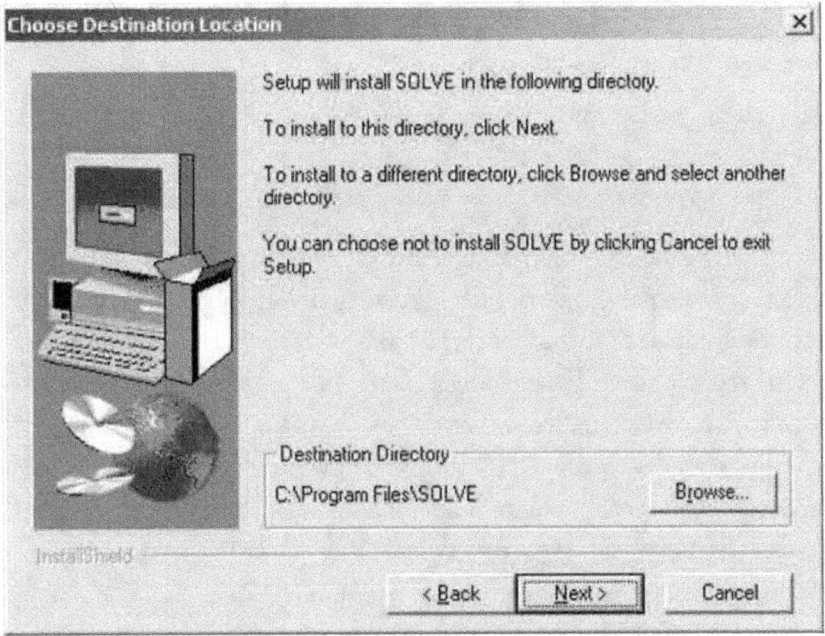

Figure 2.—The SOLVE setup routine with directory specification.

USING SOLVE
TO ANALYZE SAWMILL PERFORMANCE

In the forest products industry, the use of computerized information systems and tools is critical to business operations. In hardwood sawmills, log procurement and optimal log processing can be challenging and can critically impact the financial health of the operation. The use of computerized information systems and performance analysis applications like SOLVE can significantly improve operational efficiency. Thus, SOLVE helps sawmill managers realize the true cost and profit potential of saw logs processed in the mill (Fig. 3).

Figure 3.—SOLVE is a user-friendly computer system that helps sawmill managers improve operational efficiency and realize the true cost and profit potential of saw logs processed in the mill. Photo: U.S. Forest Service.

Data collection for SOLVE is a critical part of the analysis. If poor or insufficient data are used, the resulting reports can be misleading or incorrect. To minimize this problem, use the following systematic procedure:

- Study the layout of the mill.
- Obtain the required general data for the sawmill.
- Select, measure, and grade the study logs.
- Test run a few non-study logs through the mill to work out bugs.
- Process and collect data on the study logs.

The following five sections provide further discussion of each activity in this procedure.

STUDYING THE MILL LAYOUT

When studying the layout of the mill, keep in mind that all logs must be at least partially processed through a piece of equipment that limits production, usually the headrig. Each sawn product must be traceable to the log from which it was sawn. In small mills, the lumber inspector can probably identify the products as they are produced. For other mills, it will be necessary to write numbers or use color codes on both the logs and the sawn products. If necessary, assign people to places where they can number or code each product as it is produced. This usually requires individuals at the headsaw, resaw, edger, and trimmer. In higher production mills, two individuals may be needed at some stations.

In addition to those marking the products, several others are needed. One person is needed to post the log number or color code on a display (such as a chalk board or white board) so that crew members can identify the log being processed. Another is needed to record log sawing times. Two people will probably be needed on the green chain—one to measure and grade the sawn products and another to tally the information. An extra person also should be available to help here when needed.

Finally, one person should be available to supervise the entire operation to ensure that things run smoothly and that data are collected accurately. Also, mill situations that might affect the operation (such as slabbing logs too heavily on the headrig and edging boards too heavily on the edger) should be noted. This information can be valuable in analyzing the results.

GATHERING GENERAL SAWMILL DATA

Before deciding to perform a SOLVE analysis, make sure that certain mill information is available. First, make sure that sufficient records are available for determining reliable mill operating costs. Records also should allow you to determine actual yearly productive time versus the total yearly operating time. If you cannot get a good handle on the operating costs and times, the SOLVE economic evaluation will be of little value. But, even if this information is not available, a SOLVE evaluation can still be made. The resulting outputs give target values for log overrun, lumber yields, lumber grade yields, chip yields, and log sawing times for comparison with actual mill performance. The procedure for entering data into SOLVE is discussed in detail later (see Entering Data).

OBTAINING THE STUDY LOGS

Mill evaluations should be made with only one species at a time. After the species has been chosen, determine how many study logs are needed in each log grade (Rast et al. 1973). The log rule used can be Doyle, International ¼-inch, Scribner, or Vermont. All study logs must have scaling diameters of at least 6 inches and no greater than 30 inches. The log lengths must be at least 8 feet and less than 17 feet. Odd-length logs are acceptable.

The sampling method allows you to choose a sample size relative to the error, in dollars, that is acceptable in estimating saw log values (Table 1). You may choose the study logs at random or take them as they come from the log storage area. Isolate the study logs in an area where they can be stored until you are ready to process them. As the logs arrive, have them measured, scaled, graded, and numbered.

Table 1.—Error, in dollars, for a given average number of logs per size class

Average number of logs per size class	Error (Dollars per mbf)
2	26
3	18
4	14
5	12
6	10
7	9
8	8
9	7
10	7

Keep a dot tally of the logs by diameter and even-length classes for each log grade as shown in Table 2. Even-length classes as used here mean 8-, 10-, 12-, 14-, and 16-foot lengths. Odd-length logs are rounded down to the next even-length class. In other words, a 9-foot log would be dot tallied in the 8-foot-length class, but the length would still be recorded as 9 feet on the saw log data sheet.

Each combination of diameter and length class in Table 2 makes up a size-class cell. In other words, the 8-inch-diameter class within the 8-foot-length class makes up one cell, and the 8-inch-diameter class within the 10-foot-length class makes up another. As you dot tally the logs in these cells, periodically count the number of cells containing at least one dot. Divide this number into the total number of study logs in the grade to determine the average number of logs per size class in the sample. Then use Table 1 to estimate the maximum error that can be expected 95 times out of 100 if this sample size is used.

For example, if for a given grade and species of saw log, you have a total of 60 logs distributed over 10 cells, you have an average of six logs per size class. In Table 1, you will find an error of $10 per mbf for this sample size. This means that if you ran an analysis with this 60-log sample, the average log values in both the maximum saw log value table and the zero profit table would not be off more than $10 per mbf (95 times out of 100). This procedure should be continued until the sample size is sufficient to indicate an acceptable level of error in Table 1. An error of $10 per mbf should be satisfactory for most applications.

Table 2.—Dot tally of study logs by diameter and even-length class

Species: White Oak				Grade: 3
Diameter (inches)	**Log length (feet)**				
	8	**10**	**12**	**14**	**16**
8	8	9	8	5	1
9	5	7	12	6	
10	3		4	3	2
11		2			
12					
13					
14	1				
15			1	1	

When selecting the logs to be used in the study, do not include a few large logs in a sample of small logs. If there are only a few logs in a length class, they also should be excluded. For example, in Table 2 the log in the 14-inch-diameter class and the two logs in the 15-inch-diameter class should be excluded. The three logs in the 16-foot-length class also might be excluded. A few logs outside the prevailing size classes can have an unfavorable effect on the results by skewing the frequency distribution of the log data (which, in turn, may skew the regression results).

Grouping the logs by size class will not always be easy. In the example shown, some analysts might feel that the two 11-inch-diameter logs in the 10-foot-length class should be excluded and the three logs in the 16-foot-length class should be included. You must make these decisions based on your knowledge of the mill's typical distribution of log sizes. If in doubt about a given size class, however, include it. After the data are processed by SOLVE, the questionable log data can be checked in the SOLVE reports. These reports include graphs showing plots of both the data points and the resulting regression lines for sawing times, board foot yields, and dollar yields of the study logs. If these graphs show that the questionable log data do not fit the general trend of the other data, then remove that data and make a new computer run.

PERFORMING THE TEST RUN

Before you saw the study logs, make a test run. Make sure that the mill is in good repair and the individuals operating the various pieces of equipment are the regular operators. When your crew and the mill are ready, number a few non-study logs and have them processed through the mill. This will give you a chance to see that your crew members are positioned properly and that they know their jobs. Some adjustments may be necessary during the test run.

PROCESSING THE STUDY LOG DATA

After you have conducted the test run, you are ready to process the study logs. While collecting the data, each recorder should note any unusual occurrence that might affect the results, such as boards lost to the chipper, unnumbered boards, reasons for unusual delays, and sawing problems. This will help explain any irregularities found later. As mentioned earlier, it is important to have a supervisor watch the entire operation. The supervisor should look for milling practices that might affect overrun, lumber recovery factor, lumber grade yield, production rate, downtime, and so on. This type of information can prove valuable when the study results are analyzed (Adams 1995).

GETTING STARTED WITH SOLVE

STARTING SOLVE

To start the SOLVE application, look for the SOLVE program icon in the Windows Start menu. Keep in mind that SOLVE uses Microsoft Access to store your data. Depending on which version of Microsoft Access your computer is running, you may receive a security warning message that informs you about the usage of SOLVE's database file "Solve_ 0304.mdb" (Fig 4). Be assured that SOLVE has been tested on multiple computers and contains no deliberate malicious code that can potentially harm your computer. Therefore, you may continue starting SOLVE by clicking the *Open* button.

The flow of SOLVE is straightforward and follows four basic steps:

- Entering sawmill, log, lumber, and cost data

- Processing the data

- Providing reports

- Storing (or saving) the data to a file

Once you gather and enter the required data, SOLVE produces comprehensive reports that provide information on important operational parameters such as log size distribution, lumber grade yields, lumber recovery factor and overrun, and break-even costs.

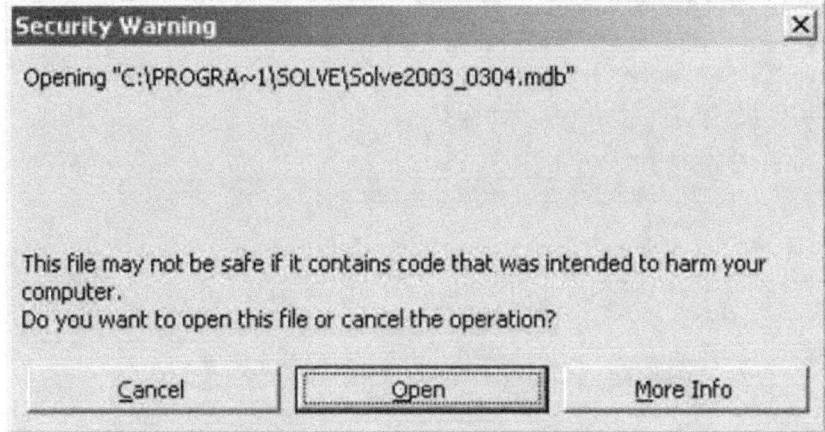

Figure 4.—The Microsoft Access security warning dialog.

BROWSING THE USER INTERFACE

The visual and functional layout of SOLVE is similar to many other Microsoft Windows programs (Fig. 5). The user interface is equipped with a menu bar that contains the application commands such as *File|Open* and *Edit|Copy*, a tool bar that contains shortcuts to selected menu commands, and a display window that shows data entry fields and report pages. SOLVE also has a navigator that contains hyperlinks for quick access to the data entry pages and report groups. This layout makes SOLVE easy to learn and follow.

EXECUTING COMMANDS FROM THE MAIN MENU

SOLVE's menu bar, as shown in Figure 5, contains a horizontal list of main menu items. Each main menu item holds a vertical list of submenus that allow you to execute commands (such as *File|Save* and *Edit|Company setup*). You can access a menu item by using your mouse or keystroke combinations. For efficiency and speed, we recommend that you use your mouse to access menu items. If you prefer to use your keyboard to select menu items, simply hold down the *ALT* key while pressing a letter that represents the underlined letter of the menu item. For example, if you wish to access the *Reports* menu, hold down the *ALT* key and then press the *R* key (uppercase or lowercase). Following is a list of SOLVE's main menu items and their basic functions.

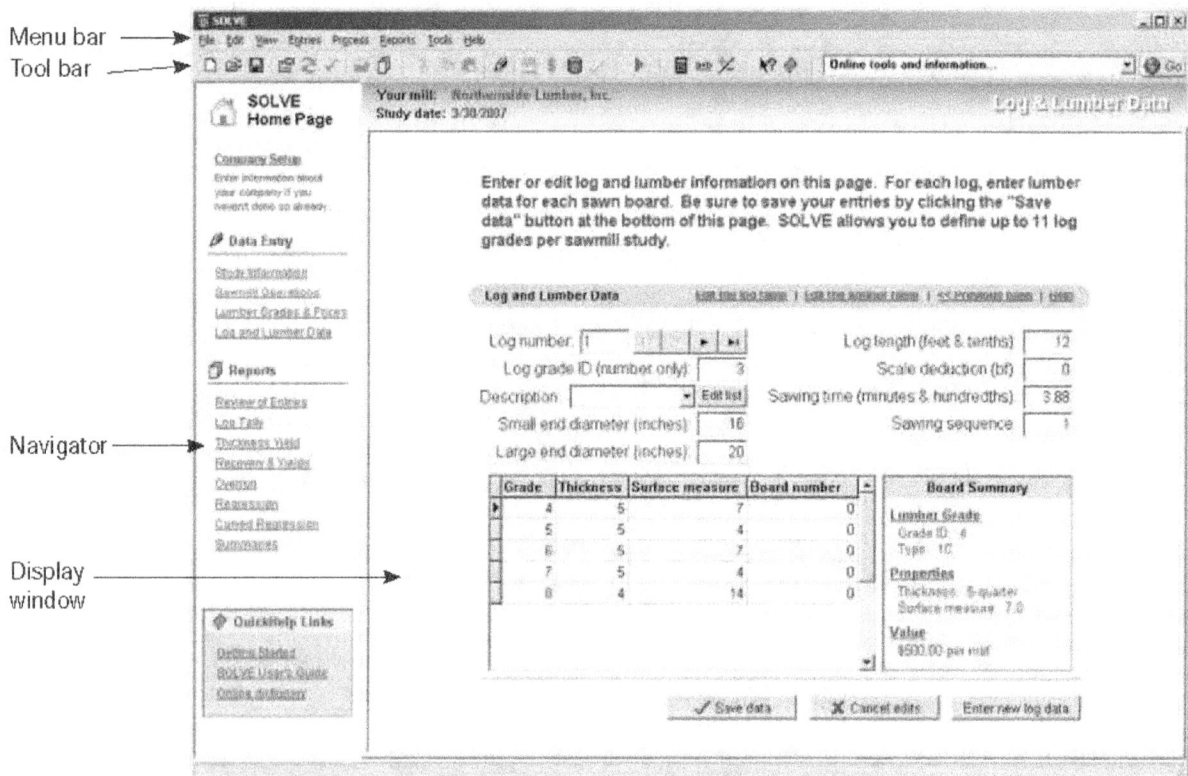

Figure 5.—The SOLVE user interface has a straightforward design that is intuitive and easy to use. The display window contains fields and tables for data entry and a section for viewing the reports.

File Menu

The *File* menu contains commands for opening, saving, importing, and exporting data files, and printing reports. Because SOLVE uses a database to store data, the tables are always populated with data even when you exit SOLVE. Thus, data from your last project will appear in the tables the next time you start SOLVE. The *Database* submenu allows you to view the database properties, refresh the database, and post (write) data to the database.

When you use the *File* menu to open a data file and you receive an *EFail Status* message, SOLVE may have encountered a database error. To work around this problem, execute *File|Database|Refresh* from the main menu. Then execute *File|Open* and re-open your data file. Finally, navigate through the submenu items from the *Entries* menu to make sure your data entry pages contain data.

Edit Menu

The *Edit* menu's standard commands are *Undo, Cut, Copy,* and *Paste* (Fig. 6). The *Company setup* command allows you to edit basic sawmill information. Finally, the *Lumber prices, Log data,* and *Lumber data* commands allow you to edit your log and lumber data tables.

View Menu

Sooner or later, you may wish to change SOLVE's on-screen appearance. You can increase the size of SOLVE's document area (the data entry pages and reports) by simply hiding the navigator, tool bar, and links bar (see Fig. 5). Conversely, you can show these

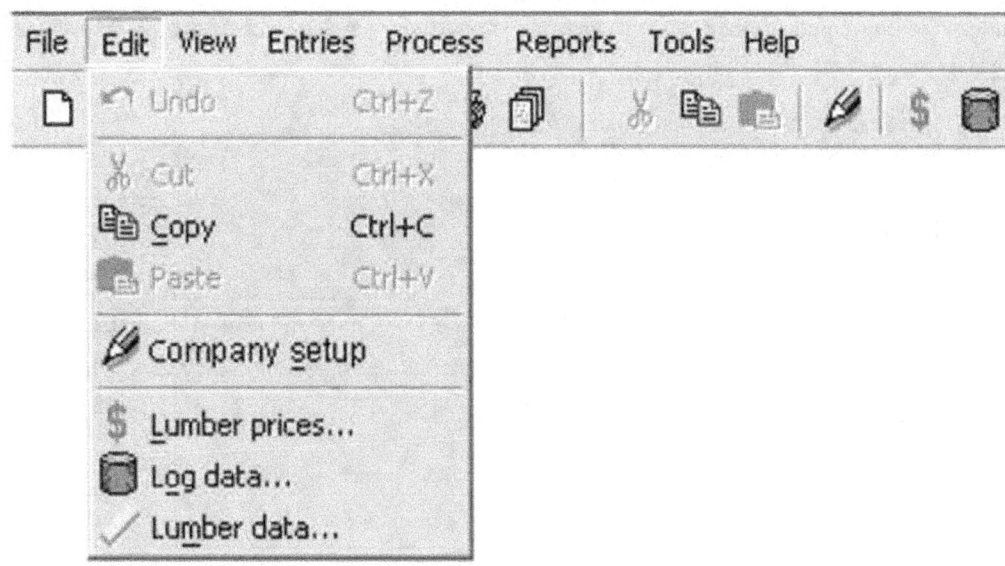

Figure 6.—SOLVE's menu can be accessed with keystroke combinations or mouse clicks. Accessing menu commands with the mouse is recommended.

objects by selecting the appropriate menu item. The *View* menu contains commands that allow you to show or hide these objects. The displayed objects are checked, while disabled objects are unchecked. These settings are stored in SOLVE's configuration file, so you will not have to reset them the next time you start SOLVE.

Entries Menu

Some users may select data entry pages by clicking the navigator links. For those who do not use the navigator, the data entry pages can be selected by using the *Entries* menu. Study information, sawmill operations, and log and lumber data pages become accessible depending on the command you select.

Process Menu

Select the *Process* menu to run your sawmill analysis. Under this menu you will see a total of nine submenu items. The use of these items is further discussed in the Running Processes section of this guide.

Reports Menu

The *Reports* menu contains a list of submenu commands for viewing the report groups generated by SOLVE. You can print these reports by selecting *File|Print the current document* or clicking the printer icon at the bottom left side of the report page. This topic is further discussed in the Viewing and Printing Your Reports section of this guide.

Tools Menu

Select the *Tools* menu if you need to use the system calculator or metric conversions utility (an external application that converts standard units to metric and vice versa). In addition, the *Application settings* submenu brings up a four-tabbed dialog box that offers file, keyboard, data directory, and help options. The *File|Options* tab provides a list that allows you to choose which default data file to open when you select *File|New*. The three options are

- Load an empty file so that I can start from scratch.
- Load the template that contains default values.
- Load the SOLVE example file.

If you are entering new data into SOLVE, select the first or second option. Select the third option if you wish to use example data to view or append your own data. Then, execute *File|New* from the menu and begin entering your data.

Some users may prefer using the Enter key to navigate between data fields. The *Keyboard Options* tab lets you specify whether the Enter (or Return) key should function as the Tab key when information is entered into SOLVE's data entry fields and tables or whether it should retain its default function as a data entry key. If you wish to use the Enter key for tabbing, select YES. If you wish to use the Tab key only for navigating between fields, select NO.

The *Directories* tab lets you specify the default directories you use for storing and retrieving your SOLVE data files, imported and exported files, and saved reports.

Help Menu

The *Help* menu contains several items that can assist you while you work with SOLVE. The first submenu item, *Getting started with SOLVE*, shows you how to immediately begin using SOLVE. The *Contents* submenu item shows the entire list of help topics while the *Current section* item shows exclusive help topics for a particular data entry page or report group. You also can access a copy of the SOLVE users guide within the *Help* menu.

VIEWING ONLINE TOOLS AND INFORMATION

If your computer is connected to the Internet, you can access tools and resources that you may find useful while working with SOLVE (Fig. 7). To access a resource, locate the *Online tools and information* drop-down field (located on the right side of SOLVE's tool bar). After selecting a resource, click the *Go* button at the right side of the drop-down field.

Figure 7.—Use the *Online tools and information* drop-down list to access tools and resources to use with SOLVE.

ENTERING DATA

On startup, the data file you worked on the last time you used SOLVE is automatically loaded. If you wish to enter a new set of data, execute *File|New* from the menu. SOLVE allows you to input data by using the data entry pages, direct edit tables, and Microsoft Excel spreadsheets (see the Direct Editing of Log and Lumber Data section for further discussion). We recommended that you use the data entry pages for entering your sawmill, log, and lumber data. Make sure that you complete all data entry fields and tables. Otherwise, SOLVE will not process your data correctly. Instead of leaving a field or table empty, enter a "0" (zero) where numeric information is required and a text value such as "none" where text-based information is required. If you are using SOLVE for the first time or working on a new sawmill study, be sure to enter your basic sawmill information using the *Company Setup* utility. Then, complete the data entry pages in sequential order (Fig. 8). Under the *Data Entry* section, start with the *Study Information* page and then progress to the *Sawmill Operations, Lumber Grades & Prices,* and *Log and Lumber Data* pages. Be sure to save your entries by clicking the *Save data* button near the bottom of each of these data entry pages, which will ensure that your changes are posted to the SOLVE database.

THE COMPANY SETUP UTILITY

If you are using SOLVE for the first time, basic information about your sawmill is required. The *Company Setup* utility (Fig. 9) allows you to enter your sawmill's name and address, information on basic sawmill operations, and names and descriptions of log and lumber grades used by your sawmill. This information is stored as default values that may be used later to fill certain fields in the *Study Information* and *Sawmill Operations* data entry pages. Log and lumber data entered under *Company Setup* will be used to populate drop-down lists on the *Lumber Grades and Prices* and *Log and Lumber* data entry pages to assist with accurate data entry. If you decide to run numerous sawmill studies, this company setup information remains constant and does not have to be re-entered for each study. If needed, you can edit your company setup data at any time. Ultimately, SOLVE uses these data to generate your output reports.

To begin your company setup, execute *Edit|Company setup* from the main menu, or click the *Company Setup* link on the navigator (if the navigator or *Company Setup* link are not visible, select the *View* menu and make sure the *Navigator, Links,* and *Company Setup* link options are checked). You will see the Company Setup dialog box and its three page tabs (Fig. 9). Enter the requested information on the *Sawmill Identification, Basic Sawmill Operations,* and *Log and Lumber Grades* pages. Following are descriptions of the pages and the data fields and tables associated with each page.

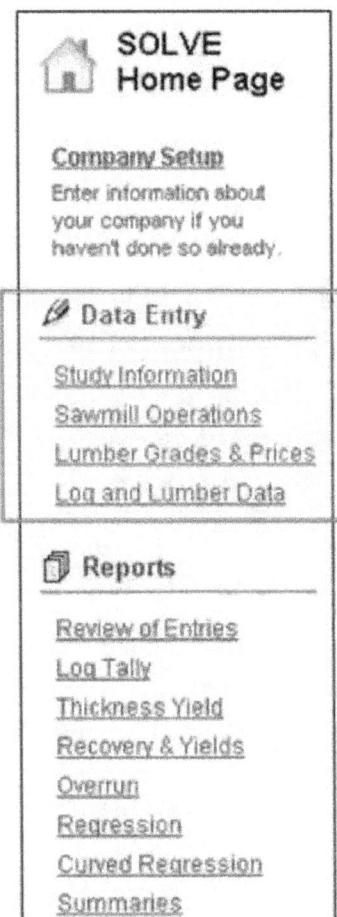

Figure 8.—After entering your basic sawmill data in *Company Setup,* enter information in sequential order, starting with *Study Information* and ending with *Log and Lumber Data* (as highlighted in this figure).

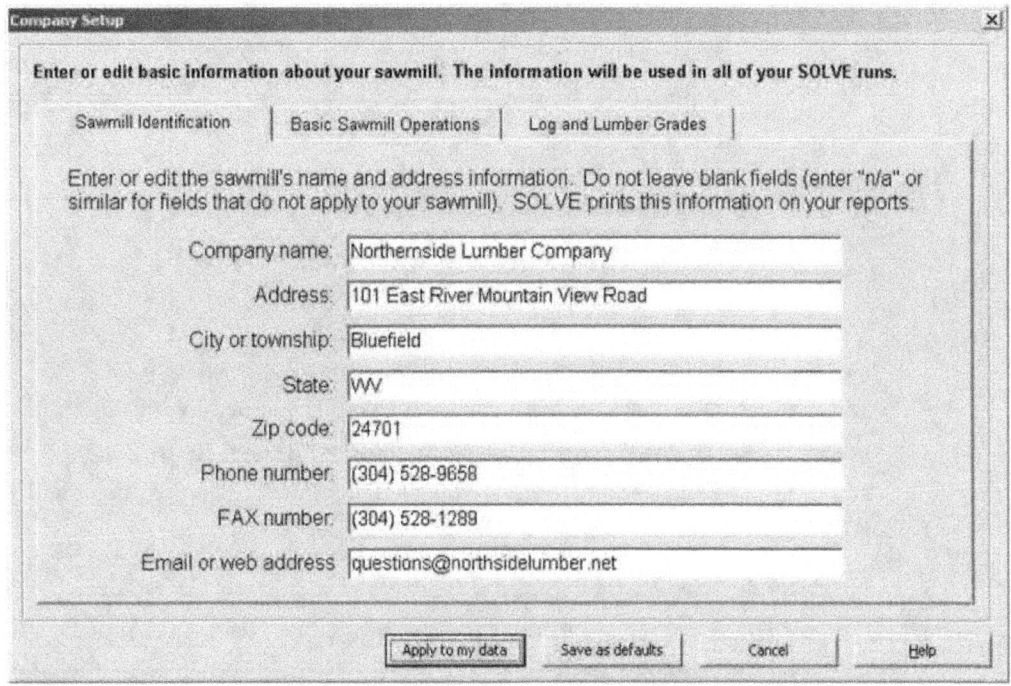

Figure 9.—Use the *Company Setup* utility to enter basic information about your sawmill. SOLVE uses this information to generate the sawmill analysis reports.

Sawmill Identification

The *Sawmill Identification* page contains eight data fields for entering your mill's name and address information. Data entry here is simple, straightforward, and optional. Even so, we suggest that you enter this information because SOLVE will print it on all of your sawmill analysis reports.

Basic Sawmill Operations

Use this page to enter important parameters from your sawmill operations. For the data fields that use percentage values, enter the value as a decimal (i.e., enter 10% as 10.00; do not include the percent symbol). The data fields on this page are

Profit margin (%) – Enter the mill manager's desired profit margin based on a percentage of expected sales (product value).

Risk margin (%) – Enter the margin that the mill manager feels is necessary to cover the risk associated with buying logs today that may not be processed for several weeks (risk of loss in value due to deterioration or change in price). This entry also is based on percentage of sales (Adams 1995).

Broker fee (%) – If you employ a broker to sell your lumber, enter the percentage of the lumber value paid to the broker for selling the lumber.

Cash discount (%) – Enter the percentage of the lumber value discounted to the lumber buyer for prompt payment (Adams 1995).

Coefficient of determination – In processing your input data, SOLVE uses statistical regression analyses to predict unknown (or unobserved) values of these six sawmill variables:

- Sawing time per log
- Lumber yield per log
- Dollar lumber value per log
- Sawing time per mbf (lumber tally)
- Lumber yield per mbf (log scale)
- Dollar value per mbf (lumber tally)

In the *Coefficient of determination* field, enter the percentage of total variation for each of the sawmill variables that is explained by the variation in log length. The regression analyses are performed for each log grade, and the values of these sawmill variables are computed by log diameter and length classes.

For example, suppose that your mill typically processes several grades of logs of various diameters and lengths of 8 to 17 feet (Fig. 10). At one particular time you process grade #1 logs with 14-inch diameters, and lengths ranging from 10 to 14 feet. The information of interest to you at this time is the number of minutes it takes to saw each of these logs (recall that sawing time per log is one of the sawmill variables). You already know the sawing time for these logs, but would like to know the sawing time for 15-, 16-, and 17-foot logs (with 14-inch diameters as well), all still within the grade #1 class. In computing the approximate sawing time per log, SOLVE examines the sawing times per log that have already been entered and uses regression routines to predict the unknown values (Fig. 10). To match any trends or variations in your data, SOLVE uses the coefficient of determination factor that you entered to compute curved, or regressed, values. In this example, if you enter a value of 0.77 into the *Coefficient of determination* field, you are telling SOLVE that 77 percent of the total variation in the sawing time per log is accounted for by the variation in log length.

The default value for the *Coefficient of determination* data entry field is 0.1. An R^2 near 0.0 indicates that the predicted value of a particular sawmill variable derived when log diameter and length are used in the equation is not much better than would be the prediction based on only the mean value of the variable for all log diameters and lengths. It further indicates an absence of a linear relationship. An R^2 near 1.0 indicates that the linear equation that includes log diameter and length calculated by SOLVE does significantly improve the ability to predict the value of the sawmill variable (Fig. 11).

Northernside Lumber, Inc.

Red Oak Study #1   Report Date: 2/20/2008 10:35:21 AM

Curved Sawing Times (Minutes per Log) by Grade
Species: Red Oak
Date of Study: 3/30/2007

Log Grade:	Diameter (inches):	Log lengths (in feet): 3	4	5	6	7	8	9	10	11	12	13	14	15	16	17
1 (Prime)																
	14	2.40	2.45	2.50	2.56	2.61	2.67	2.72	2.77	2.83	2.88	2.94	2.99	3.04	3.10	3.15
	15	2.53	2.59	2.65	2.72	2.78	2.84	2.90	2.96	3.03	3.09	3.15	3.21	3.27	3.33	3.40
	16	2.67	2.74	2.81	2.88	2.95	3.02	3.09	3.16	3.23	3.30	3.37	3.44	3.51	3.58	3.65
	17	2.80	2.88	2.96	3.04	3.12	3.20	3.28	3.36	3.44	3.52	3.60	3.68	3.76	3.83	3.91

Average per log = 3.17

Figure 10.—SOLVE uses statistical regression to predict the unknown values of a particular sawmill variable. In this illustration, the variable of interest is log sawing time per log.

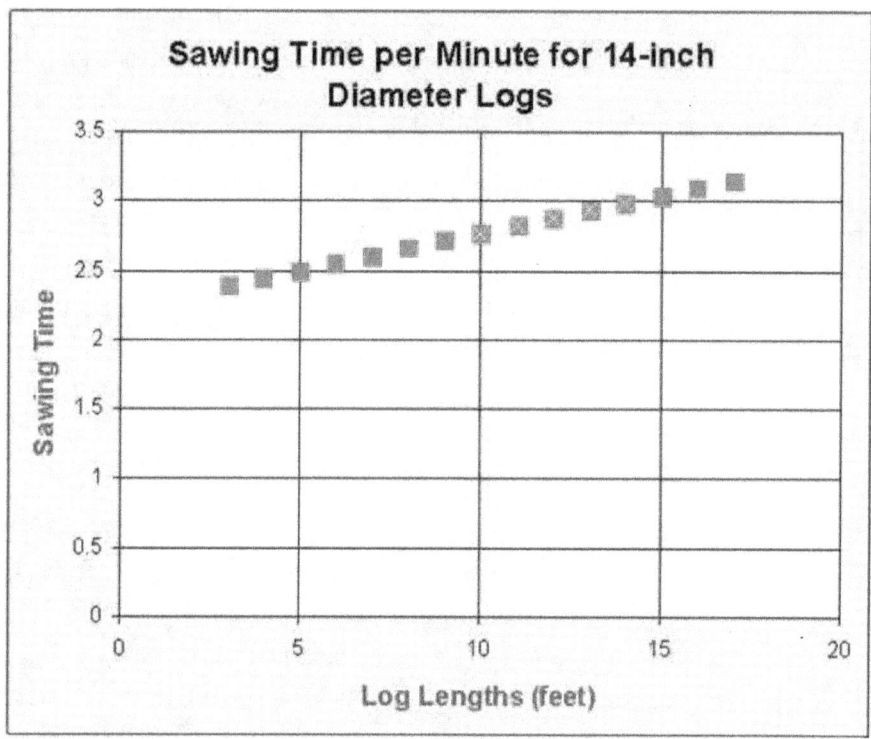

Figure 11.—SOLVE's regression routine for sawing times per log estimates the sawing time data that lie outside of the range that contains sawing times entered by the user (indicated by an X marked on the data points that lie between log lengths of 10 and 14 feet). The trend in this chart is linear and the data points show little variation. This indicates a strong relationship between log length and sawing time.

When the six regression equations are evaluated (refer back to the six sawmill variables), SOLVE compares the actual R^2 of the best-fit linear equation with the threshold coefficient of determination that you enter into this data field. If the R^2 of the best-fit equation for a regression is lower than the value you enter here, the regression equation is not used to predict the value of the variable of interest for each log length and log diameter class. Instead, the mean value for the variable of interest for all logs in a given log grade is given in all cells of the prediction tables. Although an R^2 of 0.1 (the default level) is low compared to an R^2 of 0.9, it does indicate that the calculated equation that incorporates log diameter and length improves the ability to predict the sawmill variable compared to using the mean value of the sawmill variable. Therefore, using the default value makes more sense for most analyses.

Degrade factor – Lumber value reductions can be applied to make adjustments for shrinkage and degrade losses associated with lumber drying when dry lumber prices are being used in the analysis. Other uses of this factor might exist for mills that have an integrated sorting and re-manufacturing facility where re-manufactured lumber prices would be higher, but a volume loss factor related to re-edging or re-trimming would need to be applied to relate remanufactured lumber volume and value to green lumber volume and value. Also, if re-sorting creates an offal product (e.g., thin or short lumber) that lacks a market, this volume could be factored out using this data field. Data for this field should typically be entered as a decimal that is less than or equal to 1 (which is the default value). If you enter 0.95 for example, then the realized lumber value per mbf of logs will be only 95% of the lumber price *times* the recorded lumber volume. When the lumber price entered is the price per mbf of green lumber, the degrade factor you use should be the default factor, 1.

Forcing of logs in regression – In this field you select the option that designates whether SOLVE should perform statistical regression analyses on

1. all logs in the log sample (*Force ALL logs*)
2. all logs that fall within the 95% confidence interval (CI) for the variables that are being estimated (*Delete all logs outside 95% CI*)
3. all logs in the sample in those cases where samples include fewer than 31 logs (*Force all for sample < 31*)

The third option is the default entry. If you have a high degree of confidence in the lumber data tally and log grading and scaling, then it's more sensible to use all logs in the regression analyses (option #1). If you have some doubt about the consistency and/or quality of the data, eliminating outliers using option #2 or option #3 is usually the better choice. The difference between these two options is that option #2 will eliminate from the regression analyses all logs that fall outside the 95% CI while option #3 will eliminate those logs outside the 95% CI only if there are 31 or more logs in the sample data set.

Log and Lumber Grades

This page contains two tables: the first allows you to define log grades and provide a description of each grade; the second table lets you define and describe lumber grades. For each table, enter an integer that represents the grade in the *Grade* column, enter the grade name in the *Name* column, and then enter a grade description in the *Properties* column. SOLVE stores these values so that you can select them from the appropriate drop-down fields when you enter or edit lumber and log data.

Keep in mind that SOLVE uses these data to perform a full analysis on your sawmill, so be sure to complete all of the data entry areas on each page of the *Company Setup* utility.

STUDY INFORMATION

SOLVE's first data entry page asks for information about your sawmill and the current study (Fig. 12). Click on the navigator's *Study Information* link (or select *Entries|Study Information* from the main menu) and select the *Sawmill Name & Address* tab to enter your sawmill's business name and address (address information is optional). Next, select the *Study Information* tab to enter or edit information in the *Study Description*, *Species*, *Study Date* and *Study Notes* fields. The data entry under the *Sawmill Name & Address* tab is simple and straightforward. The data fields under the *Study Information* tab, however, need a bit of explanation.

Study description – Enter any distinctive description of the current mill study. All keyboard characters, including spaces, are permitted. This data field is printed on the *Review of Entries* report and is used to distinguish between different studies conducted at the same mill.

Species – Enter the species name in this data field. Like the *Study Description* field, the species name you enter appears on the *Review of Entries* report.

Study date – Use this field to enter the date of the current sawmill study. The date information should be entered in a "mm/dd/yyyy" format. The data in this field also appear on the *Review of Entries* report.

Study notes – You can use the *Study Notes* field to record optional information about your sawmill study. This information also helps in distinguishing between

Study Information	Next page >> | Help
Sawmill Name & Address	Study Information

Study description:	Red Oak Study #1
Species:	Red Oak
Study date (mm/dd/yyyy):	3/30/2007
Study notes (optional):	This is a study for Northernside Lumber, Inc.

✓ Save data   ✗ Cancel edits

Figure 12.—The Study Information data entry form.

studies conducted at the same mill and allows you to state any special observations in your study. After entering your study information, click the *Save data* button if you wish to save your information to the database. If you do not wish to save your data, click the *Cancel edits* button.

SAWMILL OPERATIONS

The second data entry page asks for information about basic daily sawmill operations (Fig. 13). Click on the navigator's *Sawmill Operations* link (or select *Entries|Sawmill operations* from the main menu) and you will see two tabs entitled *Sawmill Operations Data* and *Advanced Entries*.

Sawmill Operations Data

Under the *Sawmill Operations Data* tab, you will see data entry fields for operating cost per minute, daily productive hours, daily operating hours, chip price per ton, log scale, log length measure, log length rounding, and chip option.

> **Operating cost per minute** – Use this field to enter your sawmill's average operating cost per minute. This figure must be determined as accurately as possible. The total cost should include all operating costs incurred by the sawmill from the log yard through lumber shipping. Make sure you include the cost for all salaries, wages, FICA taxes, employment security, workmen's compensation, group insurance, travel expenses, advertising, depreciation, interest, taxes,

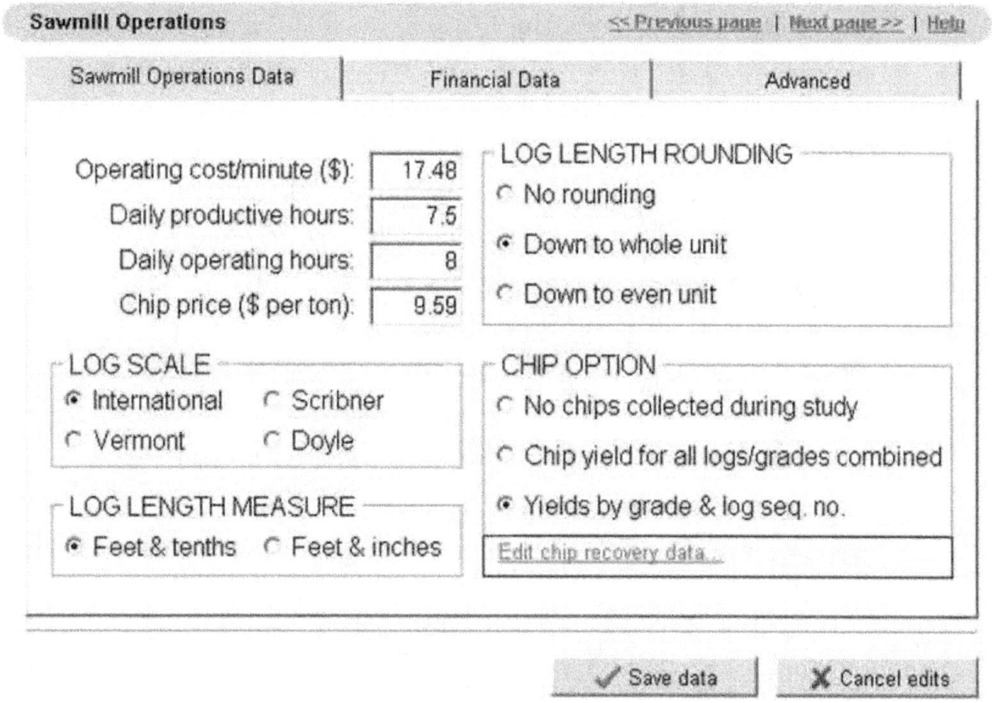

Figure 13.—The Sawmill Operations data entry form.

power, supplies, repairs, and maintenance. Do not include the broker fee for selling lumber in this cost. It is entered later. Also, make sure that you do not include the cost of saw logs or the cost of other operations not directly related to the sawmill, such as logging or hauling. If part of the overhead cost is related to other operations, prorate that part that pertains to the mill (Adams 1995).

Your entry should be a dollars-and-cents value without the dollar sign (i.e., 23.59). SOLVE uses this figure to compute sawing costs for all specified log grades. The COST program (Palmer et al. 2005) can be used to help you derive this figure.

Daily productive hours – Enter the average daily hours that the headsaw actually operates. Deductions for unproductive time such as paid breaks, scheduled maintenance, and downtime must be made to arrive at this figure (Adams 1995).

Daily operating hours – Enter the average number of hours that your sawmill operates per day. This would be 8 hours for a mill that averages 8 hours per day on a single shift and 16 hours for a mill that averages 8 hours per day for two shifts.

The total annual operating time in minutes includes the total time that the sawmill was in operation during the year. For a sawmill that works five 8-hour shifts per week, the maximum yearly operating time would be 124,800 minutes (480 minutes per day × 5 days per week × 52 weeks, where 480 minutes equals 8 hours × 60 minutes). If the mill takes a week's vacation, this figure would be reduced by 2,400 minutes (480 minutes per day × 5 weekdays). It would be reduced even further for abnormal downtime such as when the mill is closed due to extremely cold weather, fire, or major repairs (Adams 1995). Although SOLVE requires you to enter daily operating hours, this information is still useful in illustrating how non-productive time can impact the mill's total operating time.

The *Daily Productive Hours* and *Daily Operating Hours* entries are critical for successfully completing a full data processing run. These figures are used in estimating financial recovery data such as the break-even log costs and should not be overlooked. If you experience errors when running the program, check these fields to be sure you have made the correct entries.

Chip price – If chips are sold from your sawmill, enter the selling price (dollars per ton) for green chips, FOB (freight-on-board) mill. If chips are not sold, enter zero (0.00).

Log scale – Select a log scale that is used by the mill being evaluated. Your options are International ¼-inch, Vermont, Scribner (this is Scribner as opposed to Scribner Decimal C), and Doyle.

Log length measure – In this data field you designate whether your log length data is entered in feet and tenths of feet or in feet and inches. The most common way to record and enter this value is in feet and inches. The default for this data field is *Feet and inches*.

Log length rounding – You can select one of three ways of handling log lengths: *No rounding, Down to whole unit* (this is typically how log volumes are scaled for hardwood logs), or *Down to even unit*. The last choice is typically used in softwood studies because softwood lumber is usually trimmed to even lengths. Your selection here will impact both the log length distribution figures and the calculated overrun numbers because the log scale volume is affected by log length.

Chip option – If, during your mill study, you collect chips in a bin to capture the information on the weight of green chips generated during the study (or a portion of the study), you will select either *Chip yield for all logs/grades combined* or *Yields by grade and log seq. no.* Click the *Edit chip recovery data* link to define chip yields (in tons). If no chips are collected during the study, select *No chips collected during the study*.

If you select *No chips collected during study* but have a price per ton entered in the *Chip price* data field, an average chip yield figure will be used (based on studies that measured residue generation for different log diameters and lengths) to estimate the value of chips that will be recovered from the logs in the sawmill study. On the other hand, if you have not entered a chip price, SOLVE may not process the data correctly. No chip value will be given in the financial and chip reports.

If you selected *Chip yield for all logs/grades combined*, then you will need to click the *Edit chip recovery data* link to enter chip data collected for all logs in the study (using this option indicates that you collected chip yield data for the entire study but did not break the data down by log grade groups). For the chips generated during the study (for either the entire study or the log grade #1 group of logs), enter in the first data field the weight of green chip yield in tons. In the second data field, enter the number of the log that was the first log sawn during chip data collection (this will usually be log number one). The default value for this data field is zero. In the last data field, enter the number of the log that was last sawn during chip data collection. The default value for this data field is 999. You may keep the default values when processing chips using either the option *No chips collected during study* or the option *Chip yield for all logs/grades combined*.

If you selected *Yields by grade and log seq. no.*, click the *Edit chip recovery data* link to enter chip data collected for each log grade group. In the *Tons* column, enter the weight of green chips in tons. In the *Start* column, enter the number of the first log in the log grade group. In the *End* column, enter the number of the last log in the log grade group. These log grade groups must correspond with the log grades shown in the log grade/scale tally data or you will get results that are impossible to interpret (SOLVE will process the data, but the results may be illogical).

Advanced Entries

The *Advanced Entries* tab lets you enter more detailed data. In some cases, you will not have to re-enter this information each time you begin a new sawmill analysis. The *Advanced Entries* tab contains data entry fields for profit margin, risk margin, broker fee, cash discount, coefficient of determination, lumber degrade factor, and forcing of logs in regression. The default values for these data fields are located in the Company Setup utility. Instead of reentering these data for every new sawmill analysis, you can extract default values from the Company Setup data. Refer back to the *Company Setup* utility section for detailed information.

If you are not sure about what you should enter on the sawmill operation page, refer to the appropriate company records to obtain and enter the correct data. After entering your data, click the *Save data* button near the bottom of the data entry form.

LUMBER GRADES AND PRICES

Before entering your lumber grades and price data, make sure you have entered your mill information (execute *Edit\Sawmill Information* from the main menu) and have completed the *Study Information* and *Sawmill Operations* pages. Otherwise, SOLVE will not process your data correctly. To begin entering or editing lumber grades as well as the thicknesses and prices for each grade, click on the *Lumber Grades and Prices* link (or execute *Entries\Lumber grades and prices* from the main menu). Figure 14 describes the data entry fields for lumber grades and thicknesses and the price table.

Lumber grade ID – Enter into the first field an integer number for the lumber grade (e.g., 1). SOLVE allows you to enter up to 44 lumber grades.

Lumber grade description – Select a name for the current grade (e.g., FAS). You can edit the lumber grade description list by selecting the *Edit list* button (next to the *Lumber grade description* field) or by executing the *Edit\Sawmill information* command from the main menu.

Thickness type for this grade – Select the lumber thickness as either quarter measure or inch measure. For example, a thickness of 4 represents 4/4-inch-thick lumber if the thickness type is set to "QUARTER". Conversely, the thickness of 2 represents 2-inch-thick special product if the thickness type is set to "INCH". Click the *Set all to quarters button* to set all grades to quarter measure, or click the *Set all to inches* button to set all grades to inch measure.

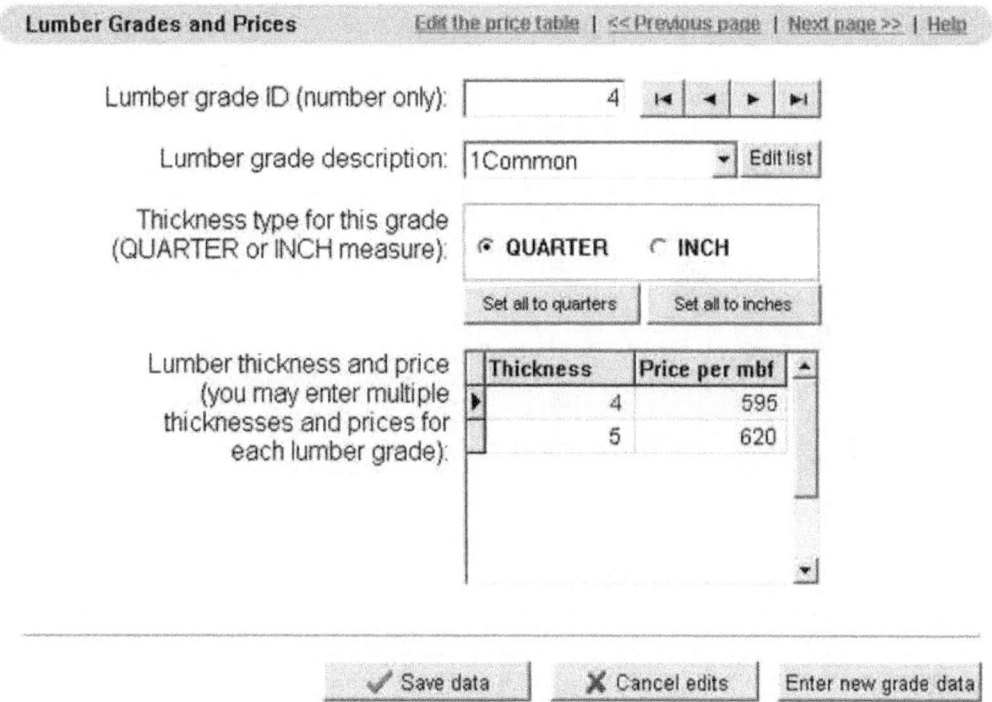

Figure 14.—The Lumber Grades and Prices data entry form.

The inch measure value is stored in whole units, so you will need to select the quarter measure option for any lumber grades for which one (or more) lumber thicknesses is not an even inch. For each lumber grade you can enter lumber size and price data in either quarter inches or whole inches, but not both.

Lumber thickness and price – This table corresponds to the current grade number and allows you to enter multiple thicknesses and prices for each grade.

After you have made your entries, be sure to click the *Save data* button to save your data to the database. If you wish to enter additional lumber grades, click the *Enter new grade data* button.

LOG AND LUMBER DATA

Again, make sure your mill information has been entered (execute *Edit|Company setup* from the main menu) and the *Study Information, Sawmill Operations,* and *Lumber Grades and Prices* pages are complete before you enter your log and lumber data. Otherwise, SOLVE will not process your data correctly. Click on the *Log and Lumber Data* link (or select *Entries|Log and Lumber Data* from the main menu) to enter or edit log data and the lumber data for each log. Following are descriptions of the data entry fields for the log data and the lumber data table (Fig. 15).

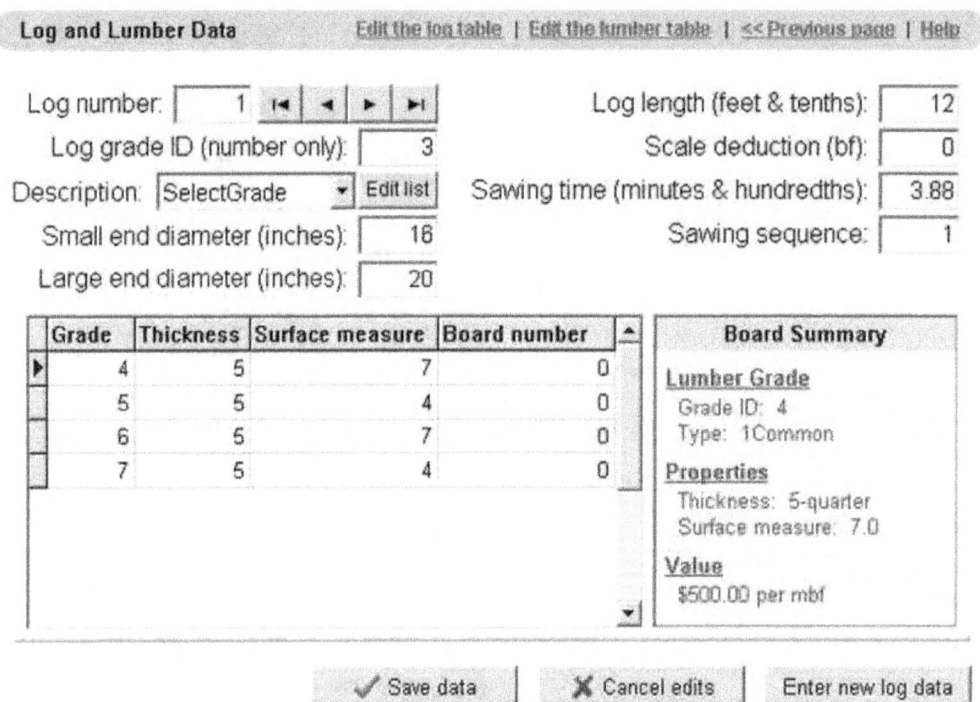

Figure 15.—The Log and Lumber Data form.

Log number – Enter an integer value in this field for the log number. Log numbers do not have to be sequentially ordered. Gaps between log numbers are okay in the log file and will not affect processing. For example, you could run a five-log study in which the logs are numbered 41, 15, 3, 111, and 13. The only problem to be aware of is that the numbers in the lumber data file must correspond with the log numbers. If you change a log number in the log file for some reason, you must also change the number in the lumber data file, or the lumber tally will not be attributed to the log from which it was sawn.

Log grade ID – Enter the integer number that represents the grade of the current log.

Grade description – Select a description of this log (i.e., prime, select). You can edit the grade description list by selecting the *Edit list* button (located beside the *Description* field) or by executing the *Edit|Company setup* command from the main menu.

Small-end diameter – Enter the average small-end diameter inside bark of the log in whole inches. This diameter is also called the *scaling diameter* of the log. For non-round logs this diameter is the average of the shortest diameter (measured through the center of the log's small-end cross section) and the diameter that is perpendicular to the shortest diameter. Therefore, round the measurements to the nearest inch. When a measurement falls exactly on the half-inch line, round down. If two measurements in a pair of measurements that are being averaged both fall on the half-inch line on the scale stick or tape, round up and down before averaging. When the calculated average diameter yields a fractional result, drop the fraction. The log diameters MUST be entered as integer values. Also, any logs with small-end diameters larger than 26 inches will be ignored in parts of the SOLVE analysis because various lookup tables used by the program are limited to 26 inches. Check your data to be sure these larger logs have been eliminated so that you do not have to deal with deciphering inconsistent numbers of logs tallied in the various reports.

Large-end diameter – Enter the average large-end diameter inside bark of the log in whole inches. This diameter is used in calculating the cubic volume of the log, an essential component of lumber recovery factor (LRF) calculations. The cubic volume formula used in SOLVE is the Smalian Formula [cubic volume = (cross-sectional area at large end of log + cross-sectional area at small end of log) / 2 × log length].

Log length – Enter the length of the log in feet and tenths of feet or in feet and inches depending on whether you selected *Feet and tenths* or *Feet and inches* in the *Log Length Measure* option field on the *Sawmill Operations* page.

Scale deduction (log defects) – Enter the scale deductions for the log in board feet and tenths of board feet. It is not uncommon during log scaling and grading to record log scaling deductions on a percent of scale-volume basis. Currently, SOLVE does not support a percentage deduction entry in this data field. Therefore, you will need to convert scale deductions to board-foot basis using a board-foot lookup table for the particular log rule that you are using. Board-footage lookup tables are included in the appendix of this document for International ¼-inch, Doyle, Scribner, and Vermont log rules.

Sawing time – Enter the sawing time of each log in minutes and hundredths of minutes. Because the goal in recording sawing time for each log is to use these times to estimate production costs for different log grades and sizes, any delays not associated with the actual sawing of the log should be recorded as downtime and excluded from the sawing time figure entered in this field. For example, a delay associated with slabs from a large log getting jammed in the headsaw outfeed system that can be attributed to log length or diameter should be included in the sawing time for a log, but a delay associated with the chipper being broken (so that slabs cannot be removed from the system) should be recorded as downtime and not included in the sawing time for a log.

Sawing sequence – Enter the sawing sequence (order of entry into mill during study) for the log as an integer. The sawing sequence list can have gaps that will not affect data processing. For example, if the log that was 193rd in the sawing sequence of a 200-log sample needs to be deleted from the data files because it has a small-end diameter larger than 26 inches, the log sequence numbers do not have to be reassigned. Neither the sawing sequence nor log numbers need to be listed in ascending order. When you process the data, the log and lumber records will be reordered by log number in the log data table.

Lumber data table (Grade, Thickness, Surface measure, Board number) – In the lower section of the Log and Lumber Data page is a table in which you will enter or edit data on the lumber recovered from each individual log. All four of these data fields should be completed with integer data entries. The table's grade and thickness values are based on data you entered in the *Lumber Grades and Prices* section (both fields are drop-downs that contain the values). Enter the surface measure of each individual board (in this case you typically will have many lumber data records per log entered in this table) or a total for all boards of a given grade and thickness that are sawn from the associated log (in which case you will have no more lumber data records per log than the number of grade and thickness combinations) in the *Surface measure* data field. Surface measures should be recorded as whole numbers. Finally, enter a board number for each lumber data record or zero (0) if the surface measure value is a total of several boards.

DIRECT EDITING OF LOG AND LUMBER DATA

If you prefer working with the log and lumber data in a table format, you can do so by executing *Edit\Log data* or *Edit\Lumber data* from the main menu. These commands will allow you to perform direct edits to the data tables (Fig. 16). Also, if your computer has Microsoft Excel installed, you can access your data tables and work with them in the form of Microsoft Excel (.xls) spreadsheets. To do this, you must first save your SOLVE data file (*File\Save* or *File\Save as*) to a directory and then open the data file in Microsoft Excel.

Unless you are familiar with your data tables, direct editing is not recommended. The data tables are linked to each other when they are opened or existent in the SOLVE database. If you attempt to change log numbers or delete logs without understanding how the tables are linked to one another, your changes may cause SOLVE to incorrectly process your data and generate inaccurate reports.

If you do not save your sawmill study data to file, SOLVE will automatically store your posted entries to the database and make them available the next time you start the application (recall that on the data entry pages, your entries are *posted*, or saved, when you click the *Save data* button). This useful feature prevents any accidental loss of data.

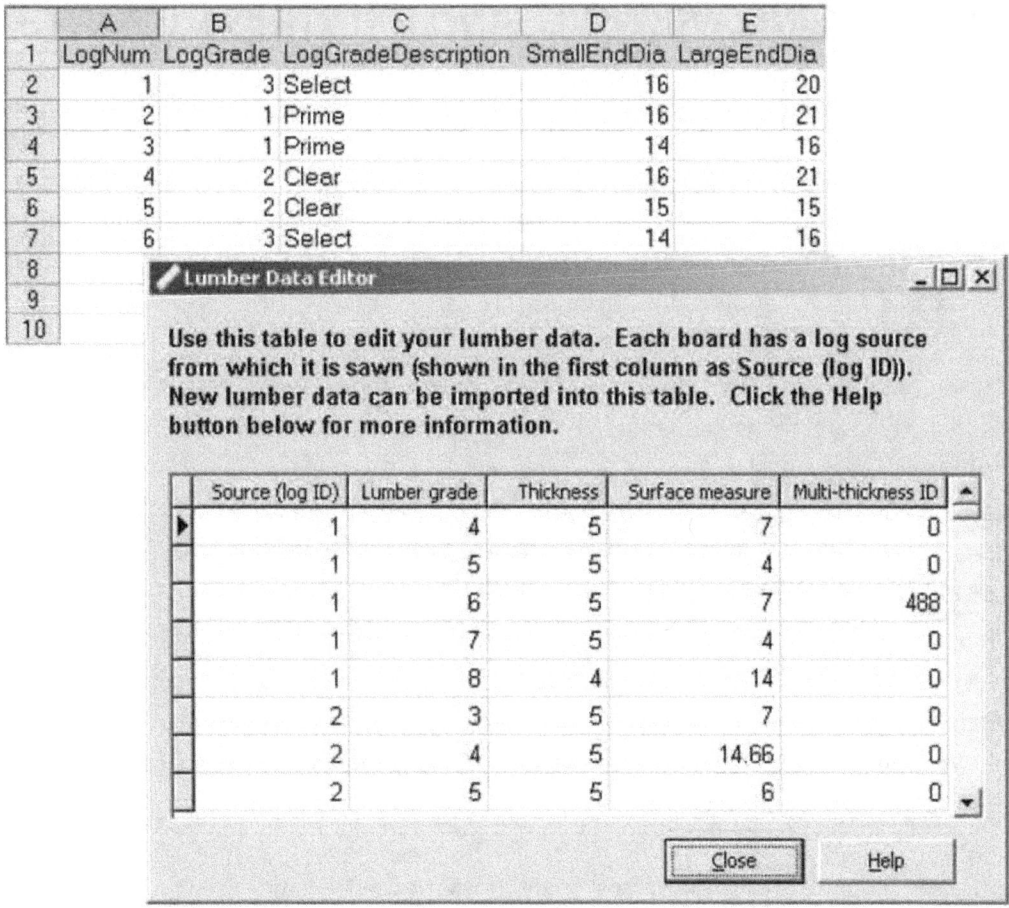

Figure 16.—You can edit your data with Microsoft Excel or the data tables provided by SOLVE. Unless you are absolutely familiar with your log and lumber data, these editing methods are not recommended.

IMPORTING DATA

You can import Microsoft Excel data files into SOLVE. If you navigate to the *DataFiles* subdirectory, you will see a list of sample files that can be imported. To import data into SOLVE, execute *File\Import* from the main menu and then select the appropriate submenu item (*Company, grades and price data, Log data,* or *Lumber data*). The data file you wish to import must be compatible with the layout of the destination table. For example, if you import a log data file, it must have the same field header names as the log data tables. Otherwise the import method will fail. Also, keep in mind that SOLVE's tables are connected (or related) to one another, so imported files must contain key fields and valid data that can be successfully linked to SOLVE's existing key fields.

PROCESSING, VIEWING, AND PRINTING REPORTS

RUNNING PROCESSES

Before you process your data, make sure you have completed all of the data entry pages. Otherwise, SOLVE will not process your data correctly. Under the *Process* menu, you will see a total of nine submenu items (Fig. 17). The first six analysis options are given in the order in which they should be processed.

Pre-process produces *Log Tally* reports for the current study. These reports are particularly useful for assessing if there are any glaring log or lumber data errors that need to be re-examined in the data (e.g., lumber yields that when summed will produce an LRF value that is infeasible). *Tally* produces the results that are shown in the *Thickness Yields* reports. *Grades* produces the results that are reported in the *Recovery and Yields* and *Overrun* reports. *Chips* produces the information in the *Summaries* reports related to chip volume and value yields. *Regressions* produces the regression, curved regression, and outlier reports. If you wish to process all of these options at once, execute *Process all data*. After processing one or all of these analysis options, be sure to execute *Generate reports* from the menu. This will ensure that the SOLVE reports are updated with your most recent entries and edits.

Selecting *Build all* is usually the most straightforward way of running the program because it processes every analysis routine at once and builds all reports. On slower computers, processing the data by stepping through the processing choices may be feasible, but on faster computers, running the entire processing step at once usually takes no longer than 45 seconds (5 seconds for data processing and 40 seconds for generating the reports) for a 200-log sample.

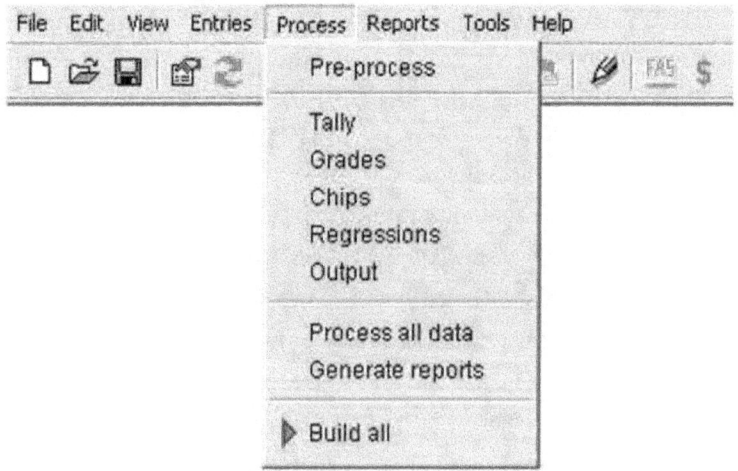

Figure 17.—Use the *Process* menu to select and run a SOLVE analysis. The *Build all* submenu item runs every analysis and generates all output reports.

VIEWING AND PRINTING YOUR REPORTS

Once your data inputs are processed, SOLVE generates eight groups of reports. The group names are listed under the *Reports* header on the navigator and under the *Reports* menu. Each report group contains individual reports that can be viewed, printed, or saved to your computer. It is important that you take a little time to review the reports in the *Review of Entries* group because they reflect the data you entered into SOLVE. If you find any errors and/or omissions, correct them and re-process your data.

To begin viewing your reports, select the *Reports* menu and choose a report group, or click a report link on the navigator bar. Then, select a report by clicking one of the links just above the report document (Fig. 18). For example, if you select *Review of entries* from the *Reports* menu, you will see a series of links near the top of the report page. Each link represents a report within the *Review of Entries* report group. Use the scroll buttons at the right side of the report screen to scroll up and down. Click on the report document to zoom in and out (your mouse cursor becomes the zoom tool that looks like a magnifying glass with a plus (+) or minus (−) sign in the center when placed over the report document). You can print these reports by selecting *File|Print the current document* or by clicking the printer icon at the bottom left side of the report page. Be advised that some reports may contain a large number of pages that could use a significant portion of your printer's memory and take a considerable amount of time to print. Therefore, make sure your printer can handle large print jobs.

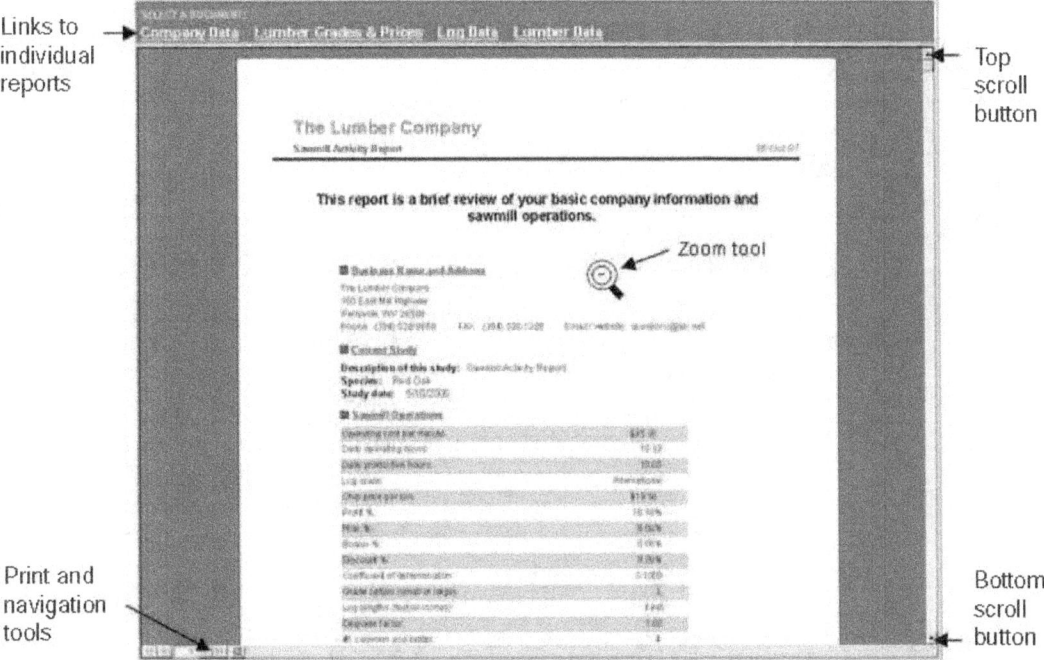

Figure 18.—The *Company Data* report is found in the *Review of Entries* report group. When you view a report, use the scroll buttons at the right to scroll up and down.

SOLVE also allows you to print a single report or a group of reports. If you are currently viewing a single report, execute *File|Print the current document* from the menu or click the print icon at the bottom left side of the report page. The *Print* dialog box will appear and allow you to select your print options. If you wish to print selected SOLVE reports, execute *File|Select reports for printing*. A multi-page dialog will appear and allow you to select any or all reports you wish to print. If you need to share a SOLVE report with others, you can save it to disk by executing *Reports|Save the current report* and selecting one of the following output formats:

- Microsoft Snapshot file (.snp) – formatted output file that can be viewed with the Microsoft Snapshot Viewer
- Rich Text Format (.rtf) – document file that can be read with a word processor such as Microsoft Word
- Web page (HTML) – hypertext markup file that can be viewed with your Internet browser
- MS Excel (.xls) – Microsoft Excel spreadsheet
- Text (.txt) – flat file with no formatting

The rich text format is a good choice for mailing files because various word processing applications can easily import .rtf documents.

ANALYZING YOUR REPORTS

As mentioned earlier, SOLVE generates eight groups of reports, with individual report documents within each group. While viewing the reports, you may notice that some contain explanatory text. Table 3 briefly describes each report.

Table 3.—The SOLVE report groups, individual reports within each group, and a description of each report

Report Group & Name	Description
Group: Review of Entries	
Company Data	A one-page report that lists all company and study-specific inputs provided by the users under the *Study Information* and *Sawmill Operations* data entry pages.
Lumber Grade & Prices	Lists the lumber price data used by SOLVE in conducting the analysis. Lumber prices are listed for each user-specified lumber grade and board thickness.
Log Data	Provides a comprehensive listing of the basic log data entered by the user in the log data entry forms. Included in this listing are log number, grade, small- and large-end diameters, length, scaling deduction, sawing time, and sawing sequence.
Lumber Data	Provides a comprehensive listing of the basic lumber data entered by the user in the *lumber data* entry forms. Included in this listing are the log number from which the lumber was sawn, the grade of the parent log, and the total surface measure of the lumber recovered from the log listed by lumber grade and thickness.

Group: Log Tally	
Log Scale (Tally Detail)	Gives a log by log tally of both the log size data and the lumber recovery data.
Log Scale (Tally)	A simplified version of the previous report. Total lumber tally per log is provided, but lumber tally by lumber grade and thickness is not detailed.
Number of Logs by Grade	A table that shows the number of logs in the study sample by small-end diameter class and log grade class.
Lengths by Grade	Shows the number of logs and percentage of logs within each log grade and small-end diameter class tallied by log length. To see additional log grade reports, select the forward arrow at the bottom left corner of the screen to advance to the next page.
Lengths ALL Grades	Like the previous report, gives the number and percentages of logs in each log length and small-end diameter class. In this report the log tally is not separated by log grade but rather a combined tally is given.
Cubic Feet by Grade	Gives log cubic footage by small-end diameter and log grade.
Group: Lumber Thickness Yields	
By Log Grade	Gives the lumber volume, expressed in board feet, recovered from logs of different grades. This lumber volume is reported for each lumber grade and thickness class.
For All Logs	Provides the same lumber volume information as in the previous report, but the data are not broken out by log grade – all log grades are compiled in a single table.
Group: Recovery & Yields	
Lumber Recovery Factor	Gives the lumber recovery factor (lumber volume in board feet divided by log volume in cubic feet) for each log grade and size (log small-end diameter) combination in the study sample.
Yields by Log Grade	Similar to the lumber thickness yield report except the lumber volume (bf) is given for each log grade, lumber grade, and log size class whereas the lumber thickness report gives the lumber volume by log grade, lumber grade, and *lumber thickness*.
Yields for All Logs	A single table in which the recovered lumber volume (by lumber grade and log size class) is given for all log grades combined.
Group: Overrun	
Gross Volume	Gives the gross log volume (before scale deductions) by log small-end diameter and log grade. The board foot volume given is for the log scale that the user indicated under the *Sawmill Operations* data entry page. However, the volume can be instantaneously switched to a different log scale by selecting an alternate scale from the choices given in the drop-down menu located above the table.
Net Volume	Gives the net log volume (after scale deductions) by log small-end diameter and log grade.
Overrun	Displays the overrun percentage for the selected log scale by log small-end diameter and log grade. The log scale can be changed using the drop-down menu at the top of the report.

Group: Regression	
Statistics	This report is quite extensive, but gives details of the regression analyses performed on the six variables of interest: sawing time per log and per mbf of lumber, lumber yield per log and per mbf of logs, and dollar value per log and per mbf of lumber. For each of the regressions, log length and log diameter are included as independent variables in the models. For each log grade, a regression report is generated for each variable. The first set of regressions (designated as Pass 1, Regressions 1 through 6) includes all logs in the sample. The second set (designated as Pass 2, Regressions 7 through 12) includes only those logs that the user has indicated are to be included; this is done when the user specifies within the *Sawmill Operations* data entry page, under the *Advanced* tab, how logs are to be handled under the *Forcing of Logs in Regression* option. If all logs are included in the regression, the *Pass 2* regression results will be the same as the *Pass 1* regression results. If all logs outside the 95% confidence interval are to be dropped from the analysis, *Pass 2* regressions may be different from *Pass 1* regressions because, in some cases, outliers may exist and these will be dropped from the analysis.
All Outliers by Log Grade	Lists all logs within each grade that are outliers for at least one of the six sawmill variables. It gives the measured and the estimated values for each of the six variables and shows whether the variable was included or excluded (1 meaning included and 0 meaning excluded) from the *Pass 2* regression runs.
All Outliers – All Log Grades	Lists the log numbers of those logs for which at least one of the six measured variables falls outside the 95% confidence interval for that variable. Unlike the *All Outliers by Log Grade* report, this list of outliers is for the regression in which all log grades are combined.
Regression Charts	Gives users the opportunity to observe a graphical representation of each of the six variables. The report's interface allows users to specify the log grade and log length they are interested in viewing (select *Edit Charting Criteria*). The charts are laid out with the variable of interest on the y-axis and log diameter classes on the x-axis.
Group: Curved Regression	
Lumber	Provides tables that give the lumber volume tally per log and per mbf (log scale) as well as the lumber value per log and per mbf (lumber tally). These values are based on the predicted values derived from the regression equations. There is a table for each log grade. Row values in these tables are the small-end diameter values of the log sample and the column values are log lengths ranging from 3 to 17 feet.
Chips	Gives the estimated (based on the regression equations) chip value per log and per thousand board feet of lumber produced, by log grade.
Product Value	Gives the estimated total product value (lumber and chips) per log and per thousand board feet of lumber, by log grade.

Sawing Times	Gives the estimated sawing time per log and per thousand board feet of log inputs, by log grade.
Conversion Costs	Gives the estimated conversion cost (based on sawing time and mill operating cost that was entered by the user in the *Sawmill Operations* section of the program) per log and per thousand board feet of log inputs.
Break-even Reports	Gives the estimated break-even price that can be paid for logs of different grades and sizes. The *Adjusted break-even log value* tables give the break-even prices (by grade) after incorporating the user-specified profit margin into the equation. The *Zero-profit log value* table gives the break-even log prices that will result in zero profit and zero loss (break-even). Thus, except in the case when a *Desired Profit Margin* of 0 is used, the *Adjusted break-even log values* will be lower than the *Zero-profit log values* because paying less for the logs will result in a profit.
Group: Summaries	
Introduction	A brief explanation of the use of the SOLVE program to support operational decisions in the sawmill.
Log Data Summary	Gives an overall summary of the logs used in the current SOLVE study including number of logs, average log diameter and length, total log volume, average overlength (trim) per log, and net volumes by log grade.
Lumber Yields	Gives an overall summary of the lumber recovery realized in the current SOLVE study including lumber volume recovered by lumber thickness, overrun and LRF for the entire set of study logs, and lumber grade recovery.
Grade Yield & Overrun	Gives an overall summary of the lumber recovery realized in the current SOLVE study by log grade and by log diameter. It also provides the percentage of lumber graded 1 Common and better by log grade and the average chip value.
Sawing Times	Shows the rate of lumber production per hour by log grade that was estimated based on the study data. The sawing rate also is presented in terms of the minutes required to saw a thousand board feet of lumber.
Financial Analysis	Shows the product value realized and average conversion costs incurred, by log grade.
Log Value and Break-even Tables	Presents the break-even log price and adjusted break-even log price (adjusted to meet required profit margin) by log grade. For a more detailed breakdown of this all important information, select the *Curved Regression* report group and then select the *Break-even Reports* link.

USING THE REPORTS TO MEASURE SAWMILL PERFORMANCE

After running your SOLVE analysis, take some time to check over the reports and make sure they do not reflect errors in your data entry (go to the report group *Review of Entries*). If necessary, navigate back to the input pages and verify that all data have been entered correctly. Then rerun your analysis.

The SOLVE reports are designed to help answer some major questions for the sawmill manager. Although the reports may have other possible uses, we will cover a few common questions:

- Is mill efficiency satisfactory?

- Are the yields by lumber grade satisfactory?

- What can the mill manager afford to pay for saw logs for a given profit and risk situation?

- What are the sawmill's break-even log sizes?

The following sections will help provide answers to these questions.

Is Mill Efficiency Satisfactory?

Two reports that help answer this question are: (1) *Recovery and Yields* and (2) *Overrun*. If you navigate to the *Recovery and Yields* report section and click on the *Lumber Recovery Factor* link, you will see the table of lumber recovery factors (calculated by dividing the board-foot lumber yield by the cubic-foot log volume). Lumber recovery factor (LRF) is one sure measure of efficiency of a mill. The table shows not only these factors by diameter for each log grade, but also average factors for each log grade and an average factor for all grades combined. When these factors are known for different mill types, the efficiency of a particular mill can be compared with that of other mills sawing similar logs and producing similar products.

Another measure of efficiency is the lumber overrun obtained by the sawmill. If you navigate to the *Overrun* report section and click on the *Overrun* link, you will see the table of overruns. Tables of percent overrun by diameter class and log grade are shown for four log rules so the mill manager can check overrun with published or known overruns even if they are shown for a log rule different from the one used by the mill. The efficiency of the mill in sawing the logs contained in the current study can be compared with that of other mills and with other log sets processed at this mill at other points in time.

If the manager finds that the mill's LRF and/or overruns are lower than they believe they should be, several things can be done. First, chip yields should be checked. If they are unusually high, check to make sure that the head sawyer is not slabbing too heavily. Next, check trimming and edging practices. If these spot checks do not pinpoint the problem, it may be necessary to set up some small studies in specific areas of the sawmill. The important thing is that the mill manager's attention has been directed to a problem area.

Are the Yields by Lumber Grade Satisfactory?

The *Recovery & Yields* report section contains several reports that show actual yields (in percent) by lumber grade and diameter class for each log grade and for all logs by diameter class. In the *Recovery & Yields* report section, click one of the links beside the *Yields by Log Grade* header (near the top of the report window). If you do not have expected yields for your log grades, but wish to compare your actual yields with another source of yield information, the Forest Service Web site contains publications with yield information on a number of different species (log on to the Forest Service's TreeSearch Web site at www.treesearch.fs.fed.us and search for *Lumber Grade Yields for Hardwood Logs*). Keep in mind that if you compare your yields with those that are published for Forest Service (FS) log grades, your study logs would have to be graded according to FS standards.

If the reported lumber grade yields seem well below expected yields, a problem may exist. First, try to explain the difference by checking the products being manufactured. Special products (such as cants) can affect the yields in some lumber grades. If the difference cannot be explained by special products, check the practices used at the headsaw, edger, and trimmer. Finally, check the log grading and lumber inspection practices.

What can the Mill Manager Afford to Pay for Saw Logs for a Given Profit and Risk Situation?

Navigate to the *Summaries* report section and click the *Log Values and Break-even Tables* report link. The *Maximum Log Value Table* (the first table in this report) shows the maximum values in dollars per mbf (log scale) for each log grade. These values indicate what the manager can pay for the logs and still make the desired profit. If you wish to view maximum values by log length and diameter, navigate to the *Curved Regression* report section, select the *Log Grade* option, and then click the *Break-even Reports* link (all are located at the top of the report window). Make sure the break-even topic in the list box shows *Adjusted break-even log value/mbf-log*.

If the manager is paying more for saw logs than the values shown in the report tables, the desired profit is not being made. To improve profitability, an attempt should be made to increase lumber recovery, reduce costs, upgrade products, or achieve some combination of these. If the manager is paying less than the values shown in the report tables, then the tables can be used as a guide for buying logs. If supply is a problem, it may be possible to pay more for logs to attract a larger supply. To improve the supply of better logs, higher prices might be paid for the better logs and lower prices paid for lower quality logs.

The maximum saw log values also can be used to show the effect that a change in mill operating costs or a change in product selling prices will have on what can be paid for saw logs. As long as the products sawn and the mill layout remain the same, the manager can change the price or cost data and rerun the original data to get updated table values. This can be done every time there is a significant change in prices or costs.

What are the Sawmill's Break-even Log Sizes?

In the *Summaries* report section, the *Log Values and Break-even Tables* report displays the *Break-even (Zero-Profit) Log Value Table* (the last table in this report). This table shows the maximum price that the mill manager can pay for each log grade and break even. Any logs showing a negative value in this table cost more to process than the value of the products obtained from them. These logs are usually found in the lower log grades, but may be found in the higher grades of low-value species. If you wish to view break-even values by log length and diameter, navigate to the *Curved Regression* report section, select the *Log Grade* option, and then click the *Break-even Reports* link (all are located at the top of the report window). Make sure the break-even topic in the list box shows *Zero-profit log value/mbf-log.*

By subtracting your current log prices from the dollar values found in the zero-profit tables, potential dollar profit or dollar loss can be found for each log size class (see the *Curved Regression* tables as explained in the previous paragraph). A zero difference, where the table value is the same as your current log price, indicates that the logs in that size class are break-even logs. A positive difference indicates the potential profit for that log size; a negative difference indicates the potential loss for that log size.

A sawmill manager usually must take the logs as they come. If the zero-profit tables, however, show that too many logs below the break-even sizes are being purchased, it may be advisable to consider adding equipment that can process these logs at a lower cost. Another option might be to investigate markets for products that will give a better return. Even if nothing can be done, it is important that the manager knows about the situation. Opportunities may develop in the future that will allow the situation to be corrected (Adams 1995).

SAVING YOUR DATA

As you work with SOLVE, we recommend that you back up your sawmill analysis data file regularly. SOLVE saves your file as a Microsoft Excel spreadsheet (.xls). To save your SOLVE data to disk, execute *File|Save* or *File|Save as* from the menu. If you wish to save individual SOLVE tables (company information, lumber grades, lumber prices, log data or lumber data), execute *File|Export* and select a table to export. Unlike previous versions, this edition of SOLVE can save and export data files to any place on your hard drive or external drive (including a USB memory stick) or to a server on a local area network (LAN).

TROUBLESHOOTING

SOLVE was written and tested on computers that run the Microsoft Windows 2000 Professional, XP Professional, and Vista operating systems. Because there are a vast number of machines with different configurations, it is virtually impossible to predict how SOLVE will behave on every machine. Therefore, we have developed a SOLVE Web site that contains solutions to common issues. Navigate to www.fs.fed.us/ne/princeton/ software/solve/support and look at frequently asked questions and other resources that may be of help. If necessary, use the SOLVE user support and feedback forms to describe any problems you may encounter while working with SOLVE.

CONCLUSION

The SOLVE computer program is the central element in a multi-faceted data collection and knowledge delivery system for sawmill operations. A second element of the system that was developed during 2000-2001 is the Cost-Of-Sawing-Timber (COST) Module, a computer-based representation of sawmill cost assessment data sheets. The COST Module produces a cost-per-minute value that is a required input for SOLVE (within the Sawmill Operations page) for calculation of profit levels and break-even log costs. Other sawmill analysis and improvement tools in the SOLVE system are detailed in *Sawmill Performance Systems for Industry: SOLVE 2000* (Wiedenbeck and Dwyer 2000). The availability of an easy-to-use sawmill study system can help mills that have not previously conducted mill studies (due to difficulties associated with data analysis and interpretation of results) to do so. The knowledge derived from these studies can help mills identify priority areas to focus on for improvements. An average 5-percent increase in sawmill value recovery per unit volume of log input is expected (Danielson and Lunstrum 1988). This will contribute to reducing demands on the eastern forest resource.

HOW TO OBTAIN A COPY OF SOLVE

The computer program described in this publication is available on request with the understanding that the U.S. Department of Agriculture cannot ensure its accuracy, completeness, reliability, or suitability for any other purposes than that reported. The recipient may not assert any proprietary rights thereto nor represent it to anyone as other than a Government-produced computer program.

You may obtain copies of SOLVE or inquire about its operation by writing:

> U.S. Forest Service
> Northern Research Station
> Forestry Sciences Laboratory
> 241 Mercer Springs Road
> Princeton, WV 24740
> Email: jpalmer01@fs.fed.us or jwiedenbeck@fs.fed.us

LITERATURE CITED

Adams, Edward L. 1995. PC-SOLVE III user's manual: a procedural guide for computer-based sawmill analysis. Gen. Tech. Rep. NE-215. Radnor, PA: U.S. Department of Agriculture, Forest Service, Northeastern Forest Experiment Station. 36 p.

Danielson, Jeanne; Lunstrum, Stan. 1988. I.M.P.R.O.V.E. system technology transfer plan. Madison, WI: U.S. Department of Agriculture, Forest Service, Forest Products Laboratory. 16 p.

Palmer, A. Jefferson; Wiedenbeck, Janice K.; Meyer, Robert W. 2005. Cost of sawing timber (COST). Gen. Tech. Rep NE-338. Newtown Square, PA: U.S. Department of Agriculture, Forest Service, Northeastern Research Station. 18 p.

Rast, Everette D.; Sonderman, David L.; Gammon, Glen L. 1973. A guide to hardwood log grading. Gen. Tech. Rep. NE-1. Upper Darby, PA: U.S. Department of Agriculture, Forest Service, Northeastern Forest Experiment Station. 32 p.

Wiedenbeck, Jan; Dwyer, Jack. 2000. Sawmill performance systems for industry: SOLVE 2000. In: Proceedings of the 2000 Hardwood Research Symposium; 2000 May 11-13; Canaan Valley, WV. Memphis, TN. National Hardwood Lumber Association: 19-29.

APPENDICES

The following four log rule footage tables can be used to convert log scale deductions (recorded as percentage of total log volume during log grading/scaling) into board footage degrade factors.

APPENDIX 1—INTERNATIONAL ¼-INCH LOG RULE FOOTAGE TABLE

Small-end Diameter (inches)	Length of Log (feet)					Small-end Diameter (inches)
	8	10	12	14	16	
	Volume (board feet)					
8	15	20	25	35	40	8
9	20	30	35	45	50	9
10	30	35	45	55	65	10
11	35	45	55	70	80	11
12	45	55	70	85	95	12
13	55	70	85	100	115	13
14	65	80	100	115	135	14
15	75	95	115	135	160	15
16	85	110	130	155	180	16
17	95	125	150	180	205	17
18	110	140	170	200	230	18
19	125	155	190	225	260	19
20	135	175	210	250	290	20
21	155	195	235	280	320	21
22	170	215	260	305	355	22
23	185	235	285	335	390	23
24	205	255	310	370	425	24
25	220	280	340	400	460	25
26	240	305	370	435	500	26

APPENDIX 2—DOYLE LOG RULE FOOTAGE TABLE

Small-end Diameter (inches)	Length of Log (feet)					Small-end Diameter (inches)
	8	10	12	14	16	
	Volume (board feet)					
8	8	10	12	14	16	8
9	13	16	19	22	25	9
10	18	23	27	32	36	10
11	25	31	37	43	49	11
12	32	40	48	56	64	12
13	41	51	61	71	81	13
14	50	63	75	88	100	14
15	61	76	91	106	121	15
16	72	90	108	126	144	16
17	85	106	127	148	169	17
18	98	123	147	172	196	18
19	113	141	169	197	225	19
20	128	160	192	224	256	20
21	145	181	217	253	289	21
22	162	203	243	284	324	22
23	181	226	271	316	361	23
24	200	250	300	350	400	24
25	221	276	331	386	441	25
26	242	303	363	424	484	26

APPENDIX 3—SCRIBNER LOG RULE FOOTAGE TABLE

Small-end Diameter (inches)	Length of Log (feet)					Small-end Diameter (inches)
	8	10	12	14	16	
	Volume (board feet)					
8	16	22	24	28	32	8
9	20	25	30	35	42	9
10	25	32	40	45	54	10
11	32	40	50	55	70	11
12	40	49	59	69	79	12
13	48	61	73	85	103	13
14	57	72	86	100	114	14
15	71	89	107	125	144	15
16	83	104	125	145	166	16
17	95	119	143	166	190	17
18	108	135	162	189	213	18
19	122	152	182	213	243	19
20	136	170	204	238	272	20
21	151	189	227	265	302	21
22	167	209	251	293	334	22
23	184	230	276	322	368	23
24	202	252	302	353	404	24
25	220	275	330	385	440	25
26	239	299	359	418	478	26

APPENDIX 4—VERMONT LOG RULE FOOTAGE TABLE

Small-end Diameter (inches)	Length of Log (feet)					Small-end Diameter (inches)
	8	10	12	14	16	
	Volume (board feet)					
8	21	27	32	37	43	8
9	27	34	41	47	54	9
10	33	42	50	58	67	10
11	40	50	61	71	81	11
12	48	60	72	84	96	12
13	56	70	85	99	113	13
14	65	82	98	114	131	14
15	75	94	113	131	150	15
16	85	107	128	149	171	16
17	96	120	145	169	193	17
18	108	135	162	189	216	18
19	120	150	181	211	241	19
20	133	167	200	233	267	20
21	147	184	221	257	294	21
22	161	202	242	282	323	22
23	176	220	265	309	353	23
24	192	240	288	336	384	24
25	208	260	313	365	417	25
26	225	282	338	394	451	26